Man the Manufacturer

by

Philip A. Sauvain

Hulton Educational Publications

Introduction

EXPLORING THE WORLD OF MAN has been designed as a series of books within the broad field of the Humanities. It is hoped that these books may prove useful in many different types of course.

The series looks at the major aspects of the work of man and most of the essential characteristics of our world civilisation, both at the present and in the past, are covered. But it is inevitable that with such a wide compass many important topics have been omitted. It is anticipated therefore that most teachers will choose to use these books as a framework within which many other studies will fit. It is also hoped that the books will prove of value in topic or 'patch' approaches to history or topic and sample-study approaches to the teaching of geography and modern studies. To cater for these differing needs there are two indexes at the back of each book – an index by time and an index by place. In this way all ten books in the series can be sampled for information on specific areas of the world or for specific periods of time.

A feature of these books is the fact that the same format for each double-page spread has been used throughout – a picture or pictures, a few interesting facts, a short passage of text, a series of assignments. It is not assumed that all the assignments will be attempted. Some will be more appropriate for some school situations than others. In addition local studies are to be found for most topics.

It is hoped that those students who work through all the books in this course will gain a world-wide picture of the evolution of civilisation and one that is not merely confined to their own country or home environment.

Contents

Stone Age Man and his Tools

Shaping an axe head

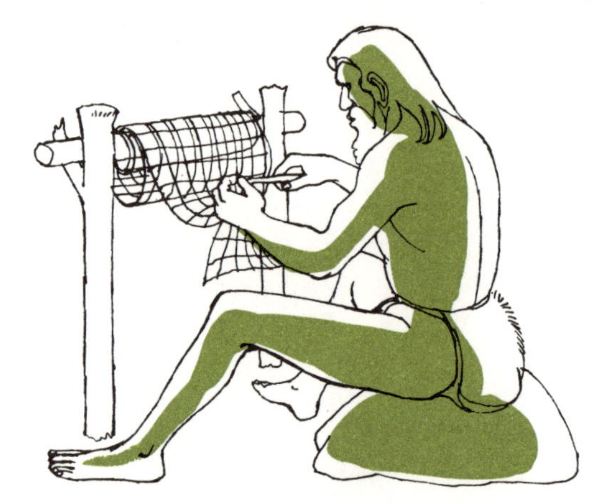

Making a fishing net

Using a burin

Sharpening a chisel

Stitching skins

Fitting a flint barb on a spear

Reading

One of the chief ways in which men differ from animals is in their ability to make and use tools. When Stone Age men first discovered that a sharp flint could be used to skin a wild animal or to carve a wooden spear they started the history of man as a manufacturer. As you can see from the drawings on the opposite page Stone Age men made a number of different tools. Some of these were used to get food with and others helped them to keep warm. Even at this time men manufactured goods from several raw materials such as axes with wooden shafts and flint heads. Man made progress slowly during this long period of time. It was only in the New Stone Age about 8000 years or so ago that change became more rapid. Even at the present day some primitive peoples know of no tools and weapons other than those made of stone, wood or antler.

Facts

★ The Stone Age men who lived about 100,000 to 10,000 years ago developed many specialised tools.

★ They even made a pointed tool, the burin, which was used to make other tools such as needles and awls. These in turn were used when stitching skins together to make clothes.

★ Stone Age men made clothes, fishing nets, bows and arrows, spears, axes, flint chisels and flint knives.

Assignments

1. Look at the pictures on the opposite page. What raw materials were needed to make the tools and the implements 'manufactured' by Stone Age man? What sources of power did he use?

2. Look at the photograph below. How did primitive man shape an axehead out of flint? Examine a stone (preferably a flint) and think out how you would set about making a tool from it without using any existing tools. (N.B. It is not wise to try to make a tool yourself. Flint-knapping is a skilled art and the unwary may be cut by sharp flying splinters of rock.)

3. Draw up a table with three columns and in the first column make a list of the tools used by man in the Stone Age. In the second column, by the side of each tool, write the name of the chief use to which the tool was put at this time. In the third column write down the names of the equivalent tools or machines which do the same job today.

Reading

In the picture on the opposite page the artist has shown how a flint mine in northern Europe might have looked like over 4000 years ago. As you can see the miners dug a fairly deep pit and extracted the flints which were embedded in the rock. They used picks made from the antlers of red deer as their tools for digging out the flints. A pole suspended over the hole enabled other miners to pull up baskets containing the flints. A rope ladder made of leather cord and wooden bars was probably their means of climbing down to the working face of the mine. As you will notice this flint mine was not greatly different in its essentials from the highly sophisticated colliery of today. The modern pit may have automatic machinery and computer control but it is still basically a hole in the ground. Men and machines cut away stone (i.e. coal) and transport it by some pulley system to the surface just as these Neolithic flint miners did so many thousand years ago.

Facts

★ At Grimes Graves in Norfolk you can still visit a number of flint mines which were worked by Neolithic miners over 4000 years ago.

★ Some of these pits were as much as 10 metres or so in depth with galleries radiating from a central shaft.

★ The flints were shaped by flint-knappers on the ground above the mines and made into axe heads and other tools.

Assignments

1. Look at the flint mine shown in the picture on the opposite page. How did the miners get down to the flint-bearing galleries? How do you think they obtained their tools? Write an account of 'a visit down a flint mine' as a Neolithic visitor might have done so 4000 years ago.

2. Describe the Stone Age tools shown in the photograph below. One is a hoe and the other is an axe. Can you tell which is which?

3. Find out when Stone Age men lived in your area. Are there any relics of those days in your nearest museum?

4. Are there any prehistoric sites dating back to the Stone Age in your district?

5. Find out whether you would be able to live off the land today if all the inventions and discoveries of the last 5000 years disappeared and you found yourself in the Stone Age. How were the tools of Stone Age man closely related to the animals and plants of his environment at that time?

Reading

The first great civilisations grew up in the Middle East in the fertile warm valleys of the Nile, Euphrates, Tigris and Indus. Here men were able to grow rich crops of corn. They also reared animals and they grew fruit. The rearing of animals such as sheep and goats and the growing of crops such as flax and cotton were prompted in part by the discovery that fibres could be used to make clothes. By drawing and twisting the fibres yarn could be made and woven into cloth which could be sold or exchanged for other goods. The farmers needed containers for their grain so that vermin could not get at it. Pots made from baked clay were excellent for this purpose and kept the grain and seed dry and safe. Pots could also be used to replace gourds made from fruit as containers for liquids – particularly wine and beer. It is interesting to see that in most civilisations pottery and weaving have been important industries just as they are in most countries today.

Facts

★ The first potters' wheels were in use in Mesopotamia about 5500 years ago.

★ The potter's wheel was a turntable linked to another wheel underneath it. As the wheel was revolved quickly by deft footwork the pressure of the potter's hand on the slab of clay on the upper wheel caused a pot to take shape rapidly and evenly.

Assignments

1. How did the potter shown in the picture opposite turn his wheel? What were his raw materials? What machines did he use?

2. Is pottery made in your area today? How is it shaped? How is it fired? How do modern methods compare with those in use in the Middle East 5000 years ago?

3. Look at the picture on this page. What industry do you think is illustrated here? Find out more about the industries of ancient Egypt and the Middle East.

4. What difference did the discovery of pottery make to the development of civilisation? What difference did the invention of weaving make? How did these developments affect the work of farmers? How did they enable men to live in the cold lands of the north?

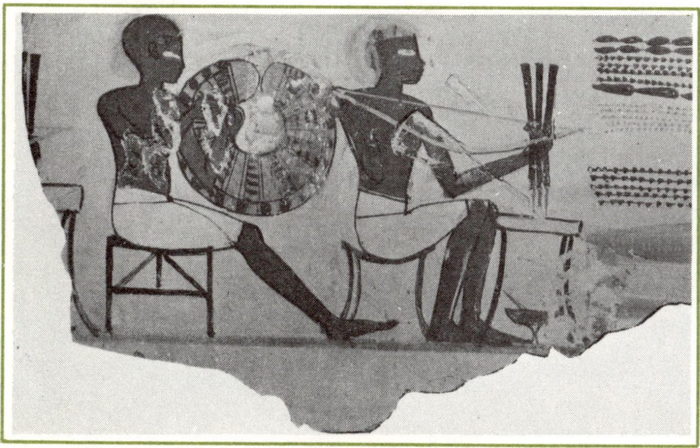

Bellows
Clay
Ore and charcoal

Reading

The first pots and cloths were manufactured during the period known as the New Stone Age or Neolithic period. This name was given because it was a time when man still relied on rocks, soil, stones, earth and timber for his raw materials. The first metal workers gained an enormous advantage over their Stone Age neighbours since they had a material which could be easily shaped and hammered or melted and cast into shapes. Knives, arrow heads, spearheads, wheels and many other products could be made from metals. The first metalworkers worked in copper, tin and bronze (the mixture of copper and tin). Gradually man discovered other alloys and other metals such as iron. The first iron workers were the Hittites who in about 2000 B.C. used iron for their swords, for their chariot wheels and for their ploughshares. At last man the manufacturer had discovered the raw material which is as important in the second half of the twentieth century A.D. as it was in the twentieth century B.C.

Facts

★ The Hittites made iron axes and could clear forested land which was uninhabitable for men equipped with weak axes of flint or bronze.

★ The Hittites could plough heavy land with their iron ploughshares.

★ Archaeologists have named the periods of early civilisation after the raw materials used by primitive manufacturers. The STONE AGE was the period of stone tools. It was followed by the BRONZE AGE and then by the IRON AGE.

Assignments

1. What parts of the chariot shown in the photograph below do you think are made from metal? How do you think primitive craftsmen shaped this chariot?

2. How do you think man first discovered he could obtain iron by smelting iron ore?

3. What prehistoric metal tools and implements have been found in your area? Are any of them on display in your local museum?

4. Find out more about the Hittites. How did they smelt the iron?

5. When were metal industries first introduced into your country?

6. Draw up a time chart to show the progress of industry in your country. On the time line indicate when the first stone and metal tools were introduced, when man first used water power, when steam engines were first introduced, and so on. Bring the history of industry up-to-date to the present time. As you read through this book you will be able to add further details to your time chart.

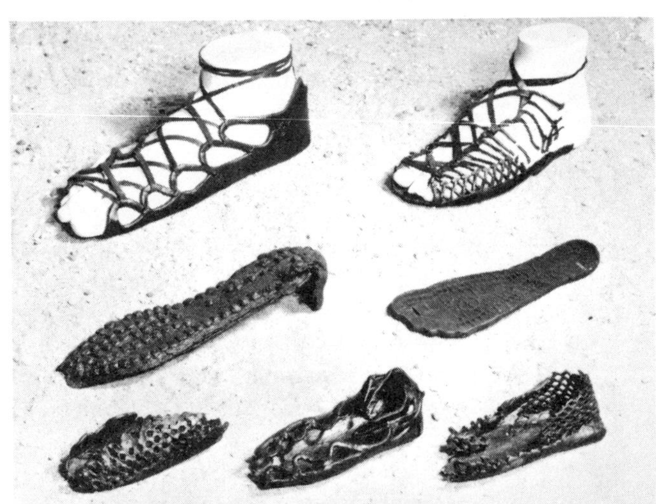

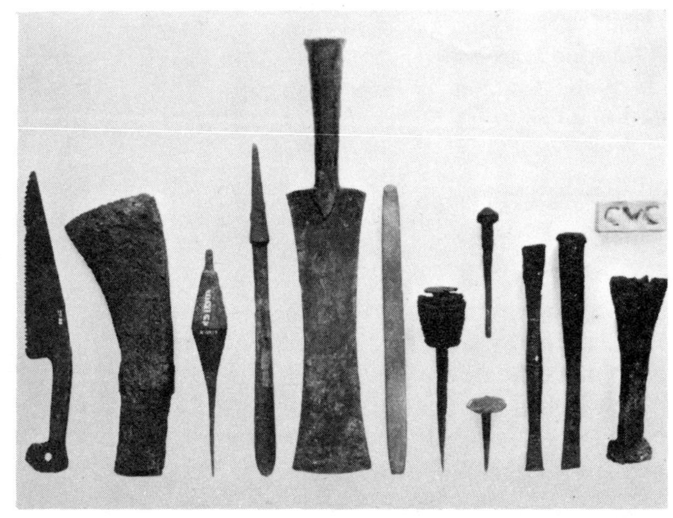

Reading

Wealthy Greek and Roman citizens lived well. Their clothes were smart, their houses comfortably furnished and their food was splendidly varied and prepared. The wealthy Roman senator living in a smart villa in Rome demanded many luxuries and comforts and there were many shops and small workshops to help supply him with these needs. A visitor to ancient Rome could have seen men manufacturing sandals, iron goods, pottery, swords, daggers, chisels, hammers, nails, ploughshares, pins, needles and countless other products. As you can see in the photographs (showing items on display in the London Museum) the Romans used cooking utensils, toiletry items, tools and other implements bearing a strong resemblance to the equivalent modern goods.

In Britain there were dyeworks at Silchester, weaving sheds at Winchester, iron mines in the Weald, copper mines in North Wales, tin mines in Cornwall and lead mines in Derbyshire. There were water mills near Hadrian's Wall (probably used to power grindstones in a flour mill) and in Northamptonshire there were pottery kilns which could fire 500 pots at a time.

Facts

★ A Roman tile in St. Albans Museum has a pawmark on it and a stone embedded close behind. It is thought that as the tile makers were taking their siesta in the sun a dog ran across the drying tiles and a workman threw a stone to frighten it away.

★ Another tilemaker disliked one of his fellow workers and left an inscription which reads: "Augustalis has been going off on his own every day for a fortnight".

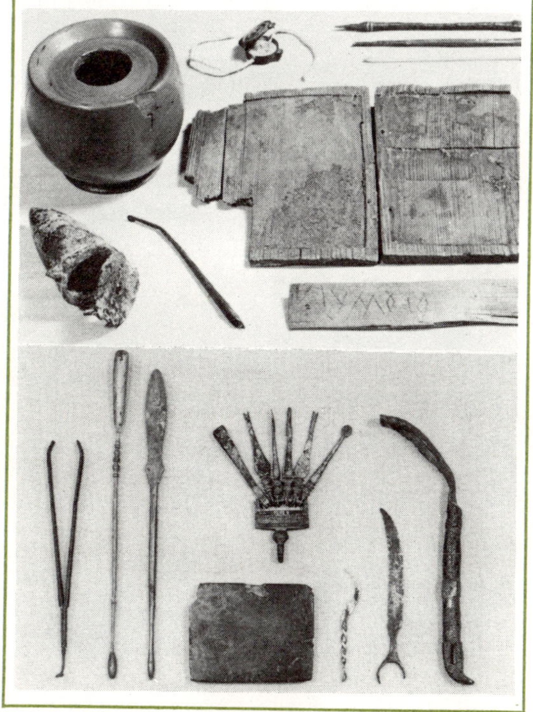

Assignments

1. What industries are represented by the Roman household goods shown in the pictures on these pages? What raw materials were needed to make these products?

2. Are there any 2000 year old tools, pots or implements in your local museum?

3. Draw a poster to advertise some of the Roman manufactures seen in the photographs on these pages. Invent suitable slogans.

4. Find out more about the industries of Ancient Rome and then write an account as if a television crew was covering a tour of Rome's industries. What things would you expect to show? What industrial processes would be seen?

5. Why do you think it is that we often seem to know most about the people of the past from their manufactures? In what ways do 'finds' of tools and pots help us to reconstruct what life was like thousands of years ago?

Industries of Medieval China

Articulated junk with explosives

Fishing reels

Chinese workshops

Reading

When Marco Polo visited medieval China about seven hundred years ago he was interested by many of the industries and manufactures he saw there. Early China had a record of achievement in science and technology unmatched by any other civilisation at the time. The Chinese were pioneers in the manufacture of paper, gunpowder and steel. They invented the compass long before the scientists of Europe. Paddle-wheel boats could be seen in China years before they were developed in the west. Chinese people were reading printed books many years before Caxton was printing books in Britain. Marco Polo was impressed by the 'stones that burned like logs' – this was coal of course and it was mined by the Chinese to provide fuel for the bath-houses in the cities. Marco Polo described their shipbuilding techniques and their use of iron nails. About 1300 years ago Chinese potters were making fine white porcelain fired at very high temperatures. This was a thousand years before potters in Europe could match the porcelain of the Chinese dynasties such as those of Sung and Ming.

Facts

★ Marco Polo saw an asbestos mine in Central Asia where the ore was crushed and washed and prepared as a fibre. The fibre was spun into yarn and woven into cloth. The asbestos cloth was then thrown into flames and emerged 'white as snow' and intact despite the fire.

★ Near the Caspian Sea Marco Polo noted gushing springs of oil which he said could be used for lighting purposes but was no good to eat.

Assignments

1. Look at the picture of the Ming vase below. Find out why Chinese porcelain is so much sought after today by collectors. What common name for good pottery recalls the subject of this section?

2. Find out whether there are any old Chinese ornaments, pictures or porcelain in your local museum or art gallery.

3. The Chinese scientists and engineers and technologists of the Middle Ages were considerably in advance of their European counterparts. Only recently has anything like the full extent of their activities been revealed. See if you can find out more about Chinese industries in the period 500 to 1500 years ago. Find out about explosives, paper, printing, clocks, compasses, silk and medicines.

4. Find out more about the industries that Marco Polo described in his "Travels" (written about the year 1300). You can probably find a copy of the "Travels" in your school library.

5. What industries could you have seen had you visited India or Japan at this time? Find out from reference books.

Reading

When the Roman Empire collapsed in Europe many Roman skills and techniques were lost. For many centuries the people of the Dark Ages continued to use iron and to weave cloth but they were simple people with little time for the elegancies and luxuries of ancient Rome. Gradually however industries developed in the towns of medieval Europe. Tradesmen manufactured goods for sale and the streets, markets and shops rang with the shouted advertisements of those days: 'Fine Satins and Stuffs', 'Velvet, Silk and Lawn'. The greatest of the medieval industries was that of woollen cloth. As you can see in the pictures on the opposite page these industries were conducted on a small scale and involved only a handful of people at a time. There were no huge sheds with hundreds of spinning wheels, looms or dye vats. The industry was well organised by guilds. These were rather like trade unions. They made regulations regarding the size and quality of the products. In this way cloth from a particular weaver could be matched by other cloth from a similar source.

Facts

★ Many old towns in Britain have streets with names recalling the medieval clothing industry and its workers. These street names include WALKER ROW and FULLER LANE (fullers), TENTER HILL (this was a frame for stretching cloth), WEBSTER STREET and WEBB LANE (weavers).

★ Other old crafts and industries are recalled by streets with names such as COALPIT LANE, FORGE ROAD, MILL LANE and SKINNERS ROW.

★ Many towns and areas in Britain were noted for their cloth such as Norfolk worsteds, Halifax cloths and Welsh friezes.

Assignments

1. Describe the medieval scenes shown in the pictures opposite. What tools and machines were used? What processes are illustrated here?

2. The photograph shows the Trinity Guildhall in King's Lynn (eastern England). What was a guildhall used for?

3. How did the medieval guilds differ from the trade unions of today?

4. What other industries were important in medieval Europe? What were some of the manufacturing achievements of the Middle Ages?

5. Look at the list below of some of the street names in British towns. What medieval industries are represented here?

Woolpack Lane	Taylor Street
The Drapery	Smithy Brow
Butter Street	Silver Street
Iron Gate	Tanner Row
Saddler Gate	Cole Gate
Potter Gate	Lister Lane
Wheeler Gate	Tenter Street
Miller Street	Colliergate
Spicer Road	Barker Street

Reading

In the picture on the opposite page you can see women weaving cloth and making pottery in an Inca village. The Incas lived in what is now the northern Andes of South America – in particular the hill lands of Peru. The Incas had developed an important civilisation by the sixteenth century and like the workpeople of the ancient lands of Africa and Asia (see page 9) they had developed the arts and skills of pottery and weaving. However the Incas had not discovered the use of the wheel and consequently their pots were shaped by hand without the aid of the potter's wheel. Weaving cotton cloth was also a fairly simple process and as you can see they used a simple loom attached to a tree or post. The cloth was woven using spindles of coloured yarns. Inca smiths used many metals and these included tin, lead and copper. In addition they worked the precious metals of silver and gold. Even so, they made little effective use of metal as a raw material, whether for tools or for implements.

Facts

★ The Maya of Central America were clever workpeople. Among other things they wove cotton cloth, manufactured velvet and produced shoes. The drawing below shows one of the beautifully designed vessels they produced about sixteen hundred years ago.

★ The Aztecs of Mexico also developed a remarkable civilisation. By the early sixteenth century they had built the splendid city of Tenochtitlan. In the markets of this city they traded products such as rubber, wood carvings and blankets.

Assignments

1. Describe the scene in the picture on the opposite page and compare it with the pictures on pages 8 and 9 showing potters and weavers in the ancient lands of the Near East. What differences are there? What are the similarities?

2. The picture on this page shows a Maya vessel of about A.D. 400. How does it compare with the Ming vase shown on page 15?

3. Make a model of the Inca industries shown in the picture opposite. Plasticine can be used as the raw material for the pots. String, wood and coloured cotton thread can be used for the loom.

4. The Central and South American civilisations of the Inca, Maya and Aztec were advanced in many ways but they did not use the wheel. How do you think this affected the way in which their industries developed?

5. How important is the use of a wheel to modern industrial processes?

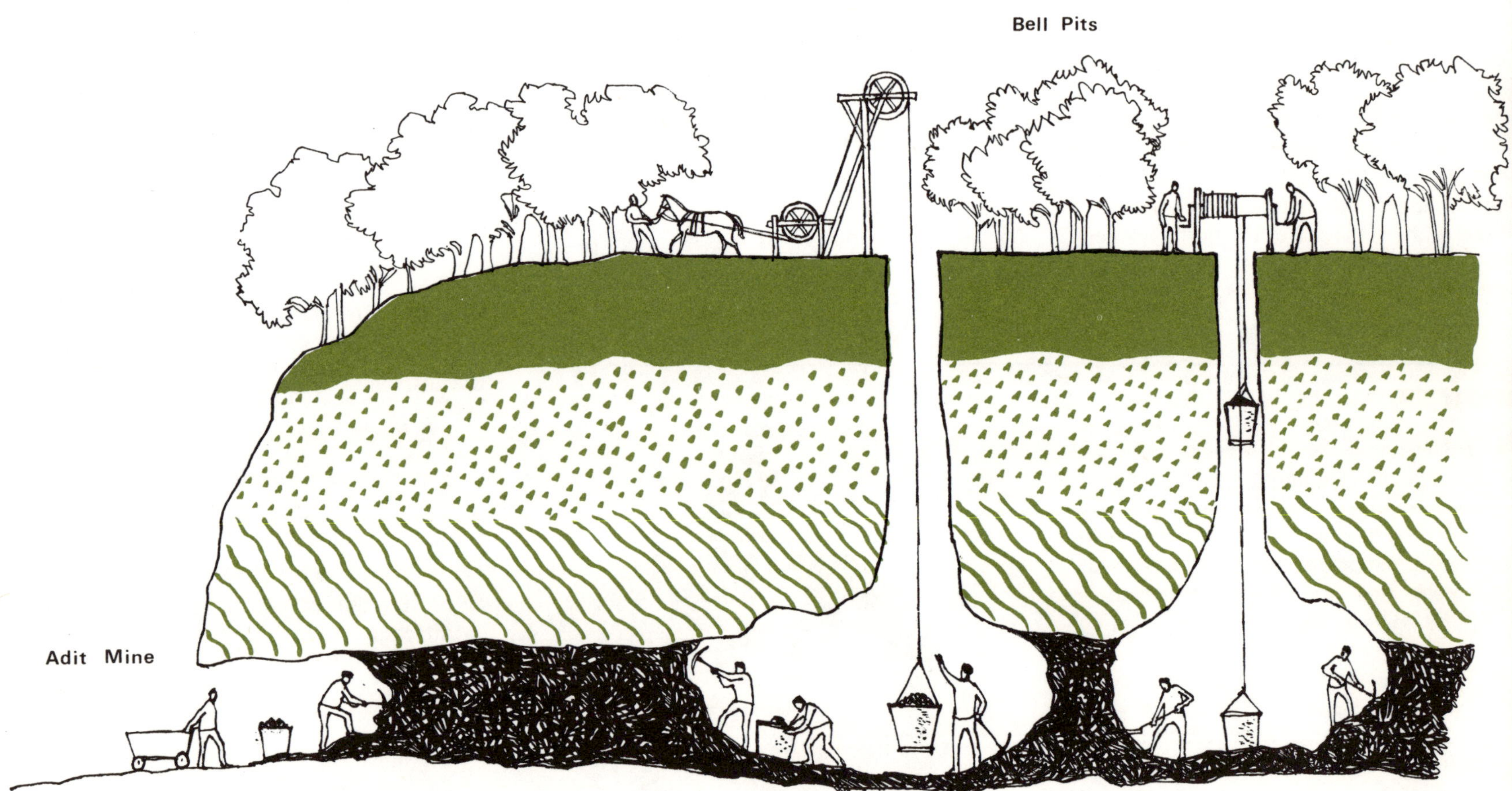
Bell Pits
Adit Mine

Reading

The picture on the opposite page makes an interesting contrast with the picture on page 6 showing a Stone Age flint mine. The coalmines of medieval Europe were of two basic types. The adit mine was where men tunnelled into the side of a hill or valley slope. They extracted the coal from the seam until they reached a point where it was unsafe to tunnel further into the earth for fear of the roof's collapsing or the presence of gas. In the other type of mine they dug out a shaft and then extracted the coal by tunnelling into the coal seams on all sides of the shaft. This type of mine was known as a bell pit and when one bell pit was exhausted as far as it was safe to do so they moved on to the adjacent land and sank another shaft. The coal was used chiefly as a domestic fuel. Londoners called it 'sea coal' because it came by sea from Newcastle-upon-Tyne. Over six hundred years ago Londoners were complaining of the smog produced by coal fires.

Facts

★ The medieval iron industry used charcoal for fuel. The iron ore and the charcoal were mixed and heated to a high temperature in a shallow furnace. Bellows were used to increase the temperature. The iron formed a hard red hot lump (or bloom) which could be hammered into shape at a forge.

★ Other heavy industries of the Middle Ages included brick-making and glass-making (see picture on this page).

Assignments

1. Describe (a) an adit mine (b) a bell pit using the picture opposite as your chief source of information.

2. What processes are illustrated in the picture below showing a medieval glassworks?

3. Make a cutaway model in plasticine of a bell pit. Make winding gear out of matchsticks and pieces of wood. Show the coal seams by using plasticine of a dark colour. Toy soldiers can be used as miners to show scale. How does the mine differ from the flint mines of prehistoric Europe (see page 6)?

4. What problems do you think the miners encountered when they burrowed into the coal seams in an adit mine? When do you think they judged it necessary to leave a bell pit? Why didn't they dig their shafts deeper? What particular item of machinery did they need before doing this?

5. How do you think man first learned that coal could be used as a fuel?

6. Why do you think the bell pit was so called?

Reading

In the picture on the opposite page you can see an ironworks situated at Kamalia in West Africa in 1790. The picture has been drawn from a description written by the explorer Mungo Park in which he gave the following details. The furnace was a circular tower of clay about three metres high and one metre in diameter. Round the base of the tower there were seven openings and in these there were tubes of clay. By controlling the flow of air into these tubes the African workers regulated the temperature of the furnace. Dry wood was put into the furnace and then covered with charcoal. Over this was laid a layer of ironstone and then another layer of charcoal and so on until the furnace was full. The fire was kindled and then blown for some time with bellows made of goats' skins. During the first day flames appeared above the furnace and burned brightly. Eventually the furnace cooled and part of it was dismantled. A large irregular mass of iron was removed and then heated in a forge and hammered into various weapons and implements.

Facts

★ In the United Kingdom there were many small forges in the woodlands where charcoal could be obtained for smelting purposes. At one forge in 1700 they needed $2\frac{1}{2}$ tonnes of charcoal and $1\frac{1}{4}$ tonnes of pig iron to make 1 tonne of bar iron.

★ When European ironworkers raised the height of their furnaces to about 10 metres and used water wheels to power their bellows they were able to raise the temperature of the ore and thus run off molten metal into pigs of cast iron.

Assignments

1. What use do you think Africans had for metals during the Middle Ages? Make a list of the tools and implements that you think they might have used.

2. Prepare an exhibit to show the scene at Kamalia as described by Mungo Park. You could draw or paint posters to show the processes involved or make a model of the furnace using card for the sides and a mixture of earth and wood for the ore and charcoal mixture. Bellows can be improvised from cardboard and a piece of cloth.

3. Trace the history of iron-making by comparing a primitive furnace such as that shown on page 10 with a modern blast furnace such as that shown on page 40. What changes have taken place? In what important respects is the modern blast furnace different from the African furnace of two or three hundred years ago? Draw a picture strip to show the history of iron and steel manufacture.

Reading

In a typical domestic industry such as the woollen and worsted industry of Yorkshire the wool was spun and prepared for weaving by one family working in their small cottage. The yarn was then woven into cloth on a loom in the cottage and eventually taken to market where it was sold and some of the purchase money used to buy wool for the next piece of cloth. A visitor to Halifax in about 1720 said that he could see cloth stretched on a tenter (a frame) outside every cottage. Each cottager had a stream nearby supplying water for dyeing the cloth and for dressing and scouring the wool. He also kept a few animals (a horse, cow, hens).

Domestic industries like this flourished in the period when handlooms and spinning wheels were the main machines of the industry. When inventors produced efficient machines for spinning and weaving wool and cotton more quickly cloth manufacturers found it profitable to build one building and have a hundred workers employed under the one roof. They did not rely, as the clothiers had done in the past, on the production of a hundred separate pieces of cloth produced in a hundred cottages.

Facts

★ In a Yorkshire clothworker's cottage six people took a week to make a single piece of cloth. They sorted the raw wool, carded it, spun it into yarn and wove it into a piece of cloth in seven days.

★ Weavers' cottages had long upper windows which threw the maximum amount of light possible into the workrooms.

★ There are still many thriving domestic industries today such as the Middle Eastern carpenter's shop seen in the photograph on the right.

Assignments

1. Describe the detailed scene on the opposite page showing a cottage industry. Draw an annotated picture of this illustration.

2. Were there any cottage industries in your area in the past? What did they produce? Are there any domestic industries in your area today (i.e. people making goods for sale in their own homes)?

3. What advantages were there in an industrial system where each cloth producer operated all the processes in his own home using his relatives as his labour force? What were the disadvantages? How do you think people brought up as independent manufacturers reacted to the introduction of steam power and machinery which could only be used on a large scale in a factory?

4. Nowadays experts talk about 'scale economies' when they point out that generally the bigger a firm gets the more efficient it becomes. Do you think this is true? Do you think all craft industries will eventually disappear?

Reading

From earliest times man tried to harness natural forces to enable his work to be carried out more effectively. He used horses and camels for transport, sails so that his ships could use the wind and from early times he used waterpower. Two thousand years ago the Romans knew how to harness the power of a river. By damming or by diverting a stream they saw that it was possible to bring water through a narrow channel (or goit) and force it to drop over a waterfall. This waterfall then created a force which could be used to turn a water wheel. Each revolution of the water wheel could be used (through a system of cogs and gears) to turn a grinding wheel (as in a flour mill or in a workshop where knives could be sharpened). The work of a water mill suffered in drought when the stream dried up. For this reason manufacturers usually preferred to build a dam and so create an artificial lake which could act as a reservoir for the water wheel and thus help to counter the effects of a dry spell.

Facts

★ The Isabella wheel on the Isle of Man is over 100 tonnes in weight and has a diameter of 22 metres. It was used for pumping water out of lead mines. (See picture opposite.)

★ Water wheels have different names according to where the water strikes the wheel. If it hits the wheel at the top it is an OVERSHOT wheel. If it hits the wheel at the bottom it is an UNDERSHOT wheel.

★ Many grindstones could be turned by one water wheel.

Assignments

1. Look carefully at the pictures of water wheels on these pages. Make a working model of a water wheel. A serviceable wheel can be made by using a mouse wheel (bought from a pet shop) and attaching pieces of card to the edges. The wheel can then be placed under a tap so that it spins freely when water is allowed to hit the wheel flaps at the top (an overshot wheel). You can imitate an undershot wheel as well and experiment to see whether there is any difference in the efficiency of the wheel in relation to the varying angles at which the water strikes the wheel blades.

2. Were water wheels ever used in your district?

3. There were disadvantages in using water power. Make a list of these disadvantages. Why do you think most manufacturers turned to steam power in the end when they had to pay for the coal and the cost of the water was negligible?

Reading

The impetus to manufacture goods in a factory came about through the development of new machines and also through the introduction of steam engines to power the machines. If more goods could be manufactured by steam-powered machines, it did not make sense to have a large number of small machines and a large number of small steam engines in a large number of cottages: one boiler house could provide steam for engines turning a number of large machines housed in the same factory. It was cheaper to make goods in this way and so manufacturers started to build mills to accommodate machines and workers. But there were problems and some of these can be seen by comparing the scenes of domestic industry (see page 24) with those of the factories on these pages. The work in a factory was often less interesting than it had been in the cottage industry. The mill owners made more money by getting their workers to do the same tedious jobs over and over again, rather than by providing a system where the worker could take a pride in his transformation of a raw material into a finished product.

Facts

★ There were many inventors in the textile industry of Britain in the eighteenth and early nineteenth centuries.

★ Kay invented the flying shuttle in about 1733.

★ Hargreaves invented a spinning jenny in about 1764.

★ Arkwright invented a water frame spinning machine in about 1770.

★ Crompton invented his mule in about 1780.

★ Cartwright invented a power loom in about 1790.

Assignments

1. Look at the pictures on these pages showing scenes in a textile factory in about 1820 and in a pen works in 1851. How would you describe working conditions in the mills in the first fifty years of the nineteenth century using these pictures as your major source of evidence? What other pictures and written accounts of early factory conditions can you find in reference books?

2. What is a factory? Discuss this topic with your friends.

3. When were the first factories built in your area? What goods were produced there? Where were the factories situated? Why?

4. Conduct an experiment with friends to show how goods can be made more efficiently on a production line than by individual craftsmen each making a product. You can use a building toy to 'manufacture' a standard product on your miniature production line.

The Coming of Steam Power

Photo: Science Museum, London

Cugnot's Steam Carriage

The Rocket

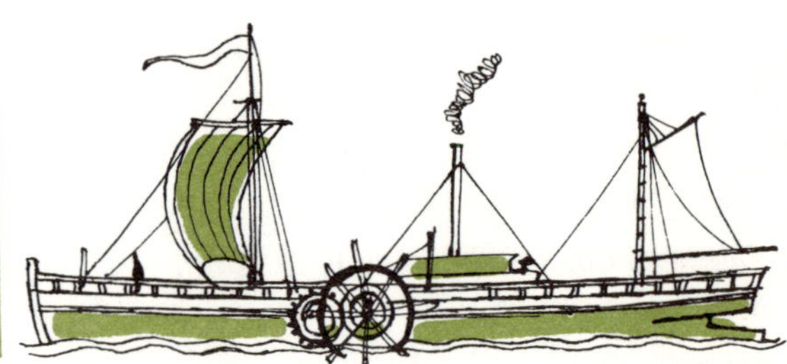

The Clermont

Reading

The most important single development in the industrial revolution of the eighteenth and early nineteenth centuries was probably the development of steam as a source of power. The pioneering efforts of Thomas Savery, Thomas Newcomen, John Smeaton and James Watt were of great importance in this field. In 1698 Savery operated a steam engine for pumping water and by 1712 Newcomen had devised a steam engine for use in the Dudley Castle colliery in the English Midlands. The engine pumped water out of the mine and was successfully produced for that purpose for most of the eighteenth century (see picture opposite). Smeaton later developed the Newcomen engine to a high degree of efficiency. Watt further developed steam engines. His designs demanded precision engineering and he was fortunate in going into partnership with a Birmingham manufacturer called Matthew Boulton. The Boulton and Watt steam engines revolutionised industrial processes in the last decades of the eighteenth century. Other engineers worked successfully in this field as well (as you can see below in the FACTS section).

Facts

★ Robert Fulton operated the paddle steamer 'Clermont' in New York State in 1807.

★ Nicholas Cugnot developed an unwieldy road steam carriage in France in 1769.

★ Richard Trevithick demonstrated a steam railway locomotive which could carry passengers at Euston (London) in 1808.

★ Horses were used in industry for a considerable period despite the coming of the steam engine.

Assignments

1. The picture on the opposite page shows a Newcomen engine in 1717 – "the engine for raising water by fire". Describe the appearance of this steam engine using the figure of the man to give scale.

2. Find out more about Nicholas Cugnot's steam carriage, Trevithick's locomotive, Fulton's 'Clermont' and Stephenson's 'Rocket'.

3. Look at the picture of the colliery in the 1790s. How did the steam engine help the miners?

4. When were steam engines first used in the factories or works of your area?

5. James Watt is popularly associated with the development of steam power. The story of Watt and the kettle is well known. In fact the early steam engines, as you have seen, had been developed long before James Watt was interested in them. Moreover they were considerably more complicated than the kettle and steam story leads us to believe. What in fact were the problems of the early steam engineers? How did their steam engines work?

Reading

The miners of 1800 earned every penny they worked for. Their hours were long, the conditions in which they worked were appalling and the dangers they faced were real, ever-present and frightening. The dangers came from poisonous fumes deep underground owing to inadequate ventilation and also to the explosive nature of methane gas which came from the coal seams. There were many pit explosions. In addition there were frequent falls of rock. Although people like Humphry Davy invented methods of minimising the risk of flames igniting the gas the safety of the miners was not secured in the nineteenth century. Apart from the dangers of catastrophic explosion there were other hardships to bear. The corridors were narrow and damp and a man might work on his back in water all day or be cramped up in a small hole. Women and children were employed in the mines and might have been seen pulling wagons and heaving sacks of coal.

Facts

★ In a British colliery disaster in 1812 well over a third of those killed were boys under the age of 16. Four of the boys were under 10.

★ In the middle of the eighteenth century British mines produced about 5 million tonnes of coal each year. A century later they were producing 60 million tonnes each year and by 1900 production had reached over 200 million tonnes each year.

Assignments

1. The picture on the opposite page shows Hetton Colliery in County Durham (England) in 1822. You can see an early railway locomotive with trucks. Describe this scene vividly as an onlooker might have done 150 years ago.

2. In the picture on this page you can see the scene at a colliery disaster in the 1880s. Find out more about the mining disasters of the past. What caused them?

3. Find pictures of mining conditions in the collieries of 150 years or so ago. Paint a poster advertising a job in a colliery in 1820 (a) as a colliery manager of the time might have done using glowing terms to describe the life (b) as we now see the terrible working conditions of those days.

4. Draw an annotated diagram of the colliery shown on the opposite page. Use arrows to highlight all the features you can recognise.

5. Write a history of mining using these pictures and those of the prehistoric flint mine (page 6), medieval coal mines (page 20) and modern mining scenes (pages 52, 53, 56).

Reading

On the opposite page you can see a typical group of millworkers in a Lancashire cotton factory in 1861. In the background you can see the mills in which they worked. At this time they would have worked long hours, six days a week and would have been poorly paid for their efforts. At 4 a.m. a millworker was woken by the 'knocker-up' rattling the bedroom window with a bunch of keys attached to the tip of a long pole. By 4.15 a.m the worker was queueing up at the factory gate. From then until 8 p.m. he was at work with little time off for refreshment. At 8 a.m. he had half an hour for his breakfast of cold tea and bread. At 12 noon he went home for a dinner of boiled potatoes and at 4.15 p.m. he had quarter of an hour for cold tea and bread again. Each year there were a few days' holiday. It was a hard life.

Facts

★ In Bradford, England, there were under 3000 power looms in 1836. Fourteen years later in 1850 there were over 30,000.

★ Conditions were appalling in the textile mills of the 1830s. There were long hours, the strap was used on sleepy children, there were frequent accidents, the work was hard and fatiguing, the atmosphere was humid and in some departments cotton dust affected the lungs. Many workers were deformed as a result of their work.

Assignments

1. The picture shows some of the workers in the Lancashire industry in the early 1860s. Can you pick out the 'knocker-up'? Describe the appearance of the mills in the background. Are there still any old mills like the one shown on this page? What advantages were there in building a mill next to a canal?

2. Are there any old mills or factories in your town? Draw a map of the district and plot the factories and mills and works by coloured dots. Use one colour to show factories which are old and ought to be demolished or replaced. Use another colour to show those you think are sensibly situated. Use a third colour to show any modern factories which are badly situated or which are ugly. When you have finished this exercise your map will show distributions of three types of factory. Does any one particular type of factory predominate in a particular area of town? Why is this?

The pastime of cycling

owes its popularity to the introduction of

DUNLOP TYRES

THE FIRST PNEUMATIC TYRE INVENTED.

OFT IMITATED, NEVER EQUALLED.

55s. per pair, guaranteed. With wired or beaded edges. Ask to see the trade mark (Dunlop's head) on cover and tube.

FOR CYCLES, MOTORS, CARRIAGES.

DUNLOP PNEUMATIC TYRE COMPANY, Limited, Para Mills, Aston Cross, Birmingham.

Ford Cars

1896

1903

A NEW KODAK.

THE No. 1A FOLDING POCKET

KODAK.

PRICE
£2 10s.

NO DARK ROOM IS NEEDED FOR CHANGING THE FILMS.

The new Kodak gives a picture 4¼ in. by 2½ in. yet is extremely light and compact. It opens and closes with one rapid movement. An eminently suitable camera for ladies, cyclists, and tourists. Write for full illustrated leaflet, post free.

KODAKS from 5s. to £7 7s

Of all Photographic Dealers, or of

KODAK, LTD., 43, Clerkenwell Road, LONDON, E.C.

Retail Branches—60, Cheapside, E.C.; 115, Oxford Street, W.; 171-173, Regent Street, W.; 59, Brompton Road, W.; also at 96, Bold Street, Liverpool, and 72-74, Buchanan Street, Glasgow.
Paris—Eastman Kodak Societe Anonyme Francaise, Avenue de l'Opera 5. Place Vendome 4.
Berlin—Eastman Kodak Gesellschaft, m.b.H., Friedrich Strasse 191. Friedrich Strasse 16.
Brussels—Kodak, Ltd., Rue du Fosse aux Loups 36.
Vienna—Kodak, Ltd., Graben 29.
St. Petersburg—Kodak, Ltd., Bolschaja Konjuschennaja 1.
Moscow—Kodak, Ltd., Petrowka. Dom Michaeloff.
Rochester, New York—Eastman Kodak Co.

J. D. Rockefeller

Reading

The great industries of the past needed something more than men, machines and inventions. They needed money. It was only money that could purchase the large machines, that could harness steam power, that could build huge factories. Inevitably some men prospered and others failed. The men who prospered built up bigger and bigger industrial empires, until in time an industry could be dominated by just a handful of names. In the United States Henry Ford was one of the early businessmen to make an enormous fortune out of motor cars. In Germany the Krupp empire was founded on iron and steel. In the United Kingdom the firm of Josiah Wedgwood developed a great pottery industry at Stoke on Trent whilst St. Helens in Lancashire thrived on Pilkington's glass. In every manufacturing town there were men of capital who built up small businesses and developed them into large companies. In the pictures on the opposite page you can see illustrations recalling a number of the men of ideas and capital of the nineteenth and early twentieth centuries.

Facts

★ J. D. Rockefeller founded the Standard Oil Company in the 1870s.

★ Andrew Carnegie made a fortune out of American railways, coal mines and iron and steel works.

★ J. B. Dunlop invented the pneumatic tyre in 1888.

★ Henry Ford founded the Ford Motor Company – one of the first to profit from the mass production of motor cars.

★ Gottlieb Daimler was an early pioneer of the motor car in Germany.

★ George Eastman introduced the Kodak box camera in the 1880s.

Assignments

1. Find out more about Rockefeller, Carnegie, Dunlop, Ford, Diesel, Benz, Daimler and Eastman. What other household names can you find by studying the history of industry in the nineteenth and early twentieth centuries?

2. Carnegie was a philanthropist with a special interest in libraries. Find out how many libraries he founded.

3. Find as many advertisements as you can featuring the names of men and women whose names are now bywords for particular products such as Ford and Daimler (cars), Dunlop (tyres) or Bell (telephones).

4. Find out more about the life of one of the great industrialists of the last hundred years or so. Imagine that you are a television producer and have been asked to make a film about the life of this industrialist. Where would you have to take your camera crew if you wanted to photograph the actual areas where the industrialist lived and worked? Did he achieve success through money, luck, hard work or genius?

Rudolf Diesel and H. Benz test the first diesel engine 1893

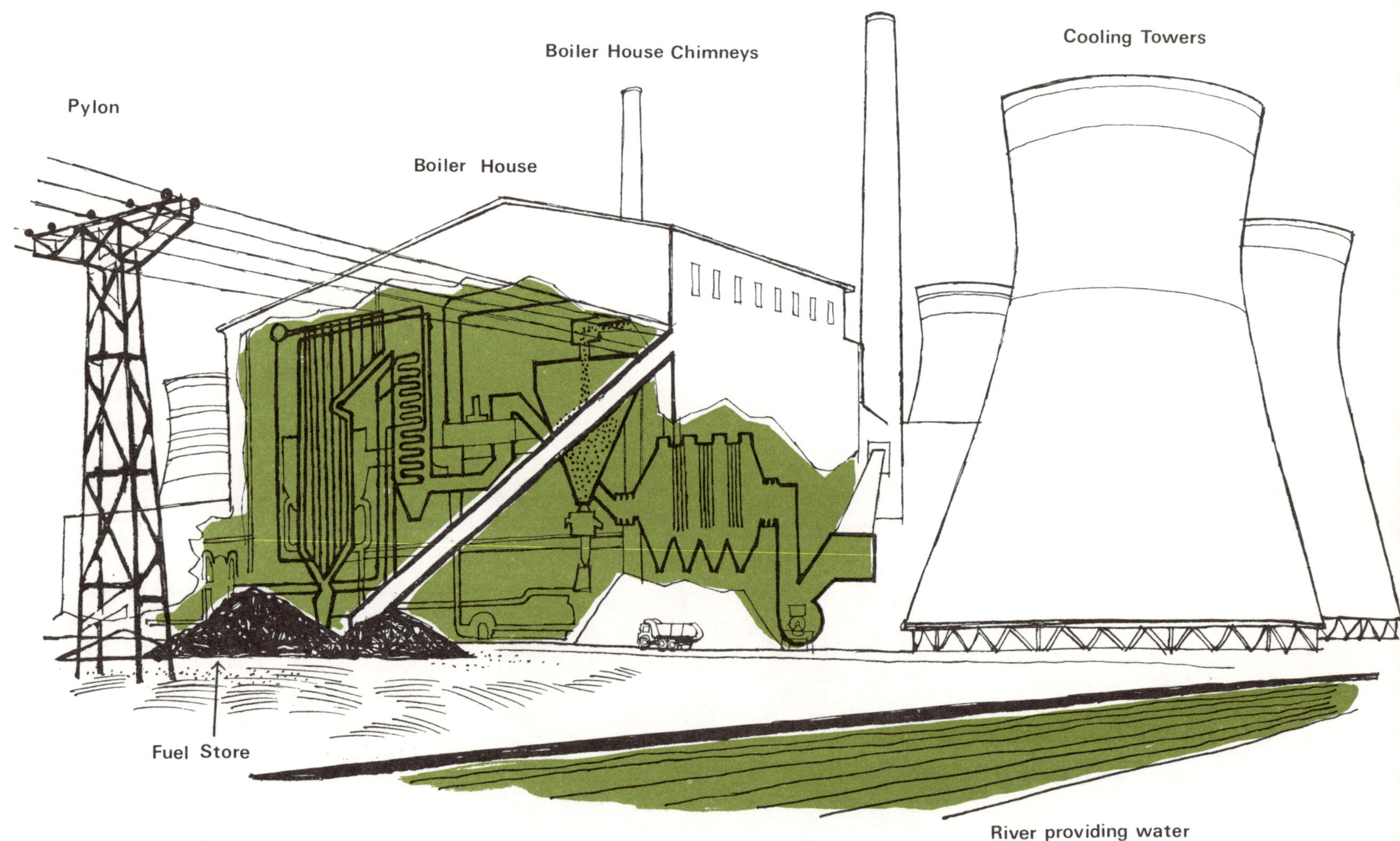
Pylon
Boiler House Chimneys
Cooling Towers
Boiler House
Fuel Store
River providing water

Reading

Successful industrial development has always depended on power. At first man used wind power to push sails and turn windmills. Then he used water power and in the eighteenth century steam power. In the nineteenth century new sources of power became available. Electricity was produced by burning coal and gas was produced by baking coke. Oil had been used for centuries but with the development of the internal combustion engine it became one of the most important sources of power available to man. Recent developments have included the harnessing of nuclear energy, although as yet the direct application of nuclear power has been limited to experimental projects such as the Russian ice breaker 'Lenin', the U.S. merchant ship 'Savannah', the U.S. aircraft carrier 'Enterprise' (with 'Nimitz' and 'Dwight D. Eisenhower' under construction), nuclear submarines and some electricity from nuclear power stations. Other sources of power have included hydro-electricity (the new use of water power) derived from the damming of streams and rivers, the harnessing of natural forces such as the volcanic springs and geysers of Iceland or New Zealand (see photograph below), and experiments in using energy from the sun.

Facts

★ The U.S.A., U.S.S.R., and China together produce nearly 70% of the world's coal. The United Kingdom produces about 9% of the total.

★ The U.S.A., and U.S.S.R. together produce about 35% of the world's crude petroleum with the Middle East countries accounting for very nearly a further 35% of the total.

★ The largest power station in the world is at Krasnoyarsk in the U.S.S.R. It can produce 6 million kilowatts – enough electricity to light five 100 watt bulbs for every person in Australia.

Assignments

1. Where is your nearest power station? Draw a field sketch showing an outline of the station and annotate it to show what each part of the building is called (the split diagram on the opposite page showing a typical power station will help you to identify these features). Where does the power station draw in its water supply? Why does it need water?

2. How are oil and natural gas brought to your country? How are they processed? How are they distributed?

3. Find out how your country's power requirements are met. How have they changed over the last fifty years or so? What are the future power requirements likely to be in the next ten years or so?

4. What are the most important sources of power used in the industries of your area? How many appear to rely exclusively on one power source? How many would be drastically affected (a) by an electricity power cut (b) by a strike of gas workers (c) by oil and petrol rationing?

The Volta Redonda Steelworks in Brazil

Reading

The earliest raw materials to be used by man when making tools and implements were stone and timber as you saw on pages 4 and 5. Modern man also uses stone and timber, despite the widespread use of metals and plastics. But as civilisation has developed the demand for new raw materials has also grown. At the same time new uses have been found for old raw materials such as the manufacture of the synthetic fibre rayon from timber. Materials which were discarded in the past are sometimes seen to have value today. The slag heaps of the South African gold mines, for instance, yield uranium ore. Without raw materials there could be no civilisation.

Of all the raw materials however, iron and steel continue to dominate the industrial development of most manufacturing nations whether they be in Europe, America, Asia, Africa or Australasia. In the pictures on the opposite page you can see steelworks in Brazil whilst on this page you can see a train (over $1\frac{1}{2}$ kilometres long) loaded with Australian iron ore.

Facts

★ The world's leading steel manufacturers are the U.S.A., the U.S.S.R., and Japan.

★ Some of the major landmarks in iron and steel production have been as follows:

1709 Darby uses coke to smelt iron ore.

1780s Cort invents the 'puddling' method for improving the quality of iron smelted in a coke furnace.

1850s Bessemer introduces his 'converter' enabling manufacturers to produce steel cheaply. Siemens develops the 'open hearth' steel making process.

Assignments

1. Look at the Brazilian steelworks on the opposite page What features can you identify? Where is the blast furnace?

2. Where is the nearest steel works to your home town? Where does it obtain the raw materials from (e.g. coke, iron ore and limestone if needed)?

3. Draw an annotated diagram to show a blast furnace. What are the chief raw materials required? Where are most iron and steel works situated? Why?

4. Find out more about each of the major landmarks in iron and steel production listed on this page. What is a Bessemer converter? What is the open hearth process? Find out more about the significant landmarks since 1850. What is the Gilchrist and Thomas process? What is an L. D. Converter? How is stainless steel produced? What new alloys contain steel?

5. Where are the important steel-producing areas of the world? Draw a map of your country to show the major steel producing regions. Show the chief sources of coal and iron ore.

Reading

If you look at the two photographs you will see a remarkable contrast between the shopfloor of the hat factory in 1909 (opposite page) and the control room of the modern chemical works (this page). In 1909 labour was cheap and there was little need to try to replace men or women by machines. Today labour is dear and manufacturers also find there are economic benefits if the manufacturing processes can be standardised and carried out by machines. The machine may sometimes be controlled by men or women. Sometimes it is controlled by computer. Fewer workpeople are needed nowadays to produce the same goods as in 1909 over sixty years ago.

Sometimes the work in a modern factory is work that involves repeating the same actions over and over again. Nowadays people look for job-satisfaction in their work. Employers and employees increasingly want the daily routine and work to be varied and interesting. It is thought that bored workers are more inclined to take industrial action than those workers who have interesting jobs.

Facts

★ In 1912 in the U.K. there were 3 million trade unionists and 41 million working days were lost through strike action. This is the equivalent of about 14 working days for each trade unionist.

★ In 1969 in the U.K. there were over 10 million trade unionists and nearly 7 million working days were lost through strike action. This is the equivalent of about 0·7 working days for each trade unionist.

★ In Australia a comparable figure for 1962 was less than 0·3.

Assignments

1. Contrast the photographs of the hat factory in 1909 and the control room in the chemical works in 1966 over half-a-century later. Account for the differences you notice.

2. Which factories in your area employ large numbers of workers? Which factories are highly automated? What type of workers do they employ?

3. What industrial disputes have affected the factories of your district in the last year or so? What caused the workers to take industrial action? Who do you think was to blame? Was it the trade unions or was it the management?

4. Look at your local newspaper and examine the advertisements for jobs in your local industries. If you do this over a period of weeks you could classify them into groups (a) by industry (b) by the types of skill required (e.g. skilled, semiskilled, unskilled). Are there any differences? Do some industries require men only or women only? Show your results in the form of a bar graph with columns proportional in height to the importance of the categories they show.

Assembly Plants

Ontario, Canada

United Kingdom

Japan

Germany

Reading

A car assembly plant is an example of a modern industry which relies on collecting together semi-finished raw materials and assembling them to form a new product. Factories of this type include vehicle plants, radio and television factories, aircraft factories and so on. In a car works the various parts which go to make up a car are assembled on a production line. The engine has its own assembly line and it starts life in a mould in a foundry where the basic casing is cast. As the engine travels down the line items such as the gear box are added. Meanwhile enormous presses create the main parts of the car body and these are welded together.

Doors are hung, the car is coated with rust inhibitors and sprayed with colour. All the interior fitments are added, such as the instrument panels, windows and the seats. Eventually the entire system is checked and the vehicle is tested before leaving the factory.

Facts

★ The world's leading motor vehicle manufacturers are the U.S.A., Japan, West Germany, France, the United Kingdom and Italy.

★ The first successful motor car to be sold in quantity was Henry Ford's Model T Ford. Over 15 million were sold between 1908 and 1927.

★ The first Model T Fords were produced at the rate of one every 12 hours. Eventually they came off the production line at the rate of one every 10 seconds.

Assignments

1. What stages of production are shown in the photographs on the opposite page?
2. The photograph on this page shows the mass production lines of colour television sets at the Yokohama plant of a Japanese firm. How do the television sets move along the production line?

3. What are the problems of running an assembly plant? What happens if one of the important constituent parts is made in another factory where there is a strike? Test out the problem of running an assembly plant by getting two or three friends to run a production line (as described on page 29). When your line is running smoothly tell one of the workers 'to go slow'. What happens to the production line? What happens if one of them stops work completely?

4. Draw a picture strip (a series of sketches) to show the manufacture of a motor car. The first picture could show the arrival at the assembly plant of a car body and the last picture could show a new car being driven away.

Reading

The twentieth century has seen a great increase in the number and variety of goods which go to make housework easier, which make life more tolerable and which cater for the leisure and pleasure interests of man. These are the non-essentials of life, however drab life without luxury may seem. These consumer goods have given rise to a massive growth in the number of factories. Television sets, radios, hi-fi sets, cameras, refrigerators, freezers, cookers, washing machines, dishwashers and mixers are just a few of the 'desirable' consumer goods of twentieth century industry. Without these goods there would be a lowered demand for steel and plastics, to name just two of the many raw materials involved. Some consumer goods are essential products in one respect and yet luxury items in another. For example, shoes are essentials, yet changing fashions may cause good shoes to be discarded long before they are worn through. Some consumer goods are made by craftsmen whilst others are mass-produced.

Facts

★ The world's leading textile producers are:

COTTON U.S.A., China, U.S.S.R., India, Japan.

WOOL U.S.S.R., U.K., U.S.A., Italy, Japan.

★ The world's leading manufacturers of radio and television sets are Japan, the U.S.A., and the U.S.S.R.

★ Many consumer goods are highly priced in relation to the cost of the raw materials of which they are made. Long-playing gramophone records are plastic discs where almost the entire value of the finished product has been added to the cheap basic raw material.

Assignments

1. The photographs on the opposite page show a German violin-maker's and a German shoe factory. On this page you can see the testing room of a Hong Kong radio factory. How far are the skills of craftsmen still needed in modern industry despite automation and computers?

2. Make a list of the consumer goods in some of your local shops which have a high proportion of their value put into them by craftsmen. To do this you can estimate the value of the raw materials and then take this away from the approximate wholesale cost of the product (which for the sake of this exercise might be estimated as $\frac{2}{3}$ the retail price).

3. Are there any craft names recalled by the surnames of the people of your town, such as Goldsmith, Cartwright, Taylor and Wheeler? What were the consumer goods of the past?

4. Which craftsmen still find that there is a great demand for their services and products? Which crafts still thrive in your district?

ARCTIC HARVESTER
CARAQUET   NEW BRUNSWICK

Reading

Food processing has always been important, from the primitive flour mills of the ancient civilisations to the computer-controlled packing plants of today. As civilisation develops, fewer people are needed to grow food. But, as more and more people get away from direct contact with the production of food, so the need for processing and packaging grows apace. Fifty years ago many housewives baked their own bread or bought loaves from a small bakery. Today the vast majority buy bread made in factories. The well-to-do housewife can order strawberries, steaks and ready-cooked meals frozen stiff and packed in polythene or foil and ready for the deep freeze. Behind this sophisticated form of shopping there is a great number of factories and food processing plants. Nowadays French table wine can be transported by railway tanker and broiler chickens are slaughtered on a production line where they stand as live animals at one end and finish ready-packed in polythene at the other. Food factories can be found in every town and increasingly farmers are turning their farms into miniature factories.

Facts

★ Scientists are busy conducting research into ways of producing palatable factory 'meat' from the proteins found in a variety of products such as timber, oil and vegetables.

★ The world's biggest producer of butter is the U.S.S.R. followed by the U.S.A., France, Germany, India, New Zealand and Australia.

★ The U.S.A. produces twice as much cheese as the world's second largest producer France.

Assignments

1. What food preservation techniques are there? When were they first introduced? How is fish preserved on board ship (see photograph opposite)?

2. What factories and works produce food or drink in your area? Which food factories just produce goods for sale in the immediate neighbourhood (e.g. milk from a local dairy)? Which factories sell their products all over the country? Which factories export their food and drink products to countries all over the world? Is there any difference between these products? How long can the food be kept before going stale or bad after leaving the factories? How does New Zealand butter (see photograph) stay fresh during the long journey to Europe?

3. Draw a picture strip to show how a food or drink product is made in your area. The first picture could show the raw material (e.g. cows being milked) and the last picture could show an advertisement for the product (e.g. butter).

4. Find out how the food and drink products of your home area are advertised. Are any of these products advertised nationally?

5. What problems of cleanliness and hygiene are there for the people who work in a food factory?

Reading

In the U.S.S.R., industrial development since 1928 has been carefully planned by stages. Successive five-year plans have helped the U.S.S.R., to make rapid industrial progress. This planned industrial development has been in marked contrast with the development of industry in countries such as Australia, the U.K., and the U.S.A. In these countries the siting and establishment of industries has been left in the main to private enterprise. In the U.S.S.R., Stalin emphasised the initial development of the heavy industries of coal and iron and steel. By the end of the seven-year plan (1959–65) the U.S.S.R., had become one of the world's leading producers of these products. Under one of the latest five year plans (1971–75) the production of consumer goods (e.g. cars, pottery, knitwear) was expected to grow more rapidly than the production of basic raw materials such as steel. Even so, the overall emphasis was still on the growth of heavy industry, with the ultimate aim of achieving standards of living comparable with those of western Europe and the U.S.A.

Facts

★ In 1965 the U.S.S.R., produced about 30 million tonnes of fertiliser. By 1970 output had nearly doubled to 55 million tonnes.

★ In 1965 350,000 tractors were produced. By 1970 the number had increased to 460,000

★ In 1940 the Soviet Socialist Republic of Kazakhstan produced 7 million tonnes of coal and 0·7 million tonnes of oil. Sixteen years later coal production had increased seven times and oil production $4\frac{1}{2}$ times.

Assignments

1. The pictures on the opposite page show various impressions of modern Soviet industry. Try to find out more about industry in the U.S.S.R.

2. Are there any industries in your area which are run by the government or which are owned by the taxpayer and not by private companies? Find out more about them and about the extent to which industry in your country has been nationalised or has been organised by the government.

3. Draw or paint a poster as a Soviet artist might do so to show the dramatic growth of Soviet industry in the year since the Revolution. What are the significant developments to emphasise?

4. What do you think are the chief advantages of having government controlled industries? What are the disadvantages? Do you think the nationalisation of industry has been successful in the countries which have so far tried it? Discuss this topic with your friends.

5. Look at reference books and try to find out where the U.S.S.R. should be placed in any list of the world's leading industrial nations.

Reading

The major fuel sources of the twentieth century include coal, oil, natural gas, hydro-electricity and nuclear energy. Of these power sources only the last two can in any way be said to be fuels that are likely to be still in use in two hundred years time. The demand for coal is decreasing each year, whilst all known reserves of oil and natural gas will have long been exhausted by that date at present rates of consumption, to say nothing of the expanding demand of a rapidly growing world population.

The future for power could lie with nuclear energy, although at the present time there has been no great breakthrough heralding the advent of nuclear power as the universal power source of the future. It may be decades before nuclear powered cars and aeroplanes are a common sight. But without nuclear energy or some other power source the world's factories will grind to a halt. Supplies of other raw materials must run out in time. Even a great lead and zinc producing centre such as Broken Hill in Australia (see photograph opposite) cannot go on producing for ever.

Facts

★ The growth in world food production has meant a decline in the ability of the land to sustain this growth. It has been estimated that half the world's cultivated land suffers from soil erosion.

★ At present rates crude oil reserves in the world should meet the demand until about the year A.D. 2000. Natural gas reserves may be exhausted before that date. Coal, on the other hand, could last as long as the year A.D. 2700 provided the consumption rate stays the same.

Mining in Ontario, Canada
Photograph courtesy Ontario House

Assignments

1. Industries have declined in the past. In 1901 there were five blacksmiths, six cloggers and five saddlers in the English town of Penrith. Seventy years later there was just one saddler. What industries of today do you think will have disappeared in seventy years time? What local industries of fifty years ago have declined in importance in your area?

2. Draw a cartoon strip to show what would happen if some raw materials ran out. You could show a world without oil or a world without steel.

3. What do you think people should do now in view of the fact that it may well be likely that future generations will have few important raw materials to work with? Discuss this topic with your friends and plan an advertising campaign using newspapers and television as the main outlets for your commercials.

4. Try to find out more about the reserves of the world's raw materials. Which materials are already in short supply?

Reading

One of the most serious problems faced by mankind at the present time is the question of industrial pollution. By pollution is meant the discharge of gases and other wastes into the atmosphere by chimneys, the creation of a mammoth litter problem through the manufacture of not-easily-disposable substances such as plastics and the discharge of noxious effluent and other matters into the rivers and into the seas. This problem is having an effect on health, on foods and on natural life. It is increasingly difficult to find ways of disposing of the marvellous products that have been fashioned from the earth and its resources. The problem of disposal comes about partly through the inability (or the reluctance) of the manufacturer to make products which could have an indefinite life. The eternal razor blade, the everlasting electric light bulb and the indestructible motor car are just a few manufacturing daydreams. The problems of a polluted atmosphere have also given rise to concern, whether from factory chimneys, car exhausts or supersonic aircraft.

Facts

★ A supersonic airliner releases about 1 tonne of carbon dioxide during a two-hour flight.

★ Over 1 million trees died in an area about 100 kilometres away from the smogs of Los Angeles.

★ In Tokyo about 300 grammes of soot and dirt fall on each square metre of the city every year. At this rate 6 tonnes of soot and dirt would have collected on each square metre in the period since the time of the Romans!

Assignments

1. The pollution of the atmosphere is almost inevitable in some industries, however modern and up-to-date the machinery. Look at the photograph of the modern chemical works in Germany on the opposite page. Do you think the many advantages we obtain from chemicals (drugs, textiles, fertilisers) are worth the amount of pollution produced by a factory of this type?

2. The photograph below shows a zinc smelter set amid fine mountains in British Columbia in Canada. What are the problems of siting industries in areas of beautiful scenery? Should we be prepared to do without the products and the prosperity in order to have unspoiled scenery, or is it more important to provide employment and make use of the resources available?

3. Are there any factories or works in your area situated in pleasant surroundings? Do the factories spoil the landscape or have they been designed to blend in?

4. Do any local factories or works pollute your home area? Find out about the state of your local rivers. See if you can get information about the air you breathe.

Zambian Copper Mines

Reading

Industrial growth has not been confined to the highly developed communities of Europe, North America, the U.S.S.R., Japan and Commonwealth countries, such as Australia. Industry is booming in places as diverse as Kenya, Chile and Thailand. In some countries minerals and other natural resources such as water power are exploited. New hydro-electricity schemes like the Volta River Project in Ghana have provided cheap power for industries. One example is the smelting of bauxite to produce aluminium. Sometimes the industries have developed out of agricultural or plantation produce, such as the rubber industry of Malaysia or the jute industry of Bangladesh. These industries partly process raw materials for export to the major industrial areas of the world. Some industries have developed with an eye on world markets but others have grown to meet the local demand for consumer goods. As new industries are introduced living standards in the developing countries rise and the new 'wages' stimulate the building of even more new factories.

Facts

★ One of the most important recent discoveries in the developing nations has been the finding of large reserves of oil in African countries – Libya and Nigeria, for instance.

★ In the 1960s India prepared plans for the construction of nuclear power stations.

★ The widespread growth of the world iron and steel industry in the 1960s is illustrated by the fact that steel works have been established in Chile, Egypt, Pakistan, Burma, Thailand and Malaysia.

Indian Textile Workers

Assignments

1. What contribution do you think ordinary people can make to the welfare of developing countries? Why do you think many people say that it is better to supply the tools and finance to support industries rather than provide food to allay the pressing food problems of today? Discuss this topic with your friends.

2. What industries do you think a developing country should try to start first of all? Should it be heavy industries (e.g. steel or chemicals) which provide raw materials or should it be light industries providing some of the basic requirements of twentieth century living?

3. Make a study of the daily newspapers and weekly magazines and find out what references they contain to industries in the developing countries.

4. What advice would you want to offer people in a country which has not had a history of industry and now seeks to establish manufacturing industries of all kinds? What mistakes did the industrialists of Europe, the U.S.A., and the U.S.S.R., make in the past?

New Sources of Power

left: Using a computer in the Israel Institute of Technology
right: Nuclear Physics Department of the Weizmann Institute, Israel

Reading

As you have already seen, fuels such as coal, oil and natural gas have only a limited life. Many people put their faith in nuclear energy as a source of power for the future (see page 39). However, a different type of power is making great progress. In the 1800s machines replaced men in many mills and skilled handloom weavers were replaced by weavers 'minding' power looms. In the 1970s computers are also replacing men. This time it is clerks and other white collar workers who are being replaced as much as industrial workers on the shop floor. A computer can perform thousands of calculations in seconds. This is a new and subtle use of power. A computer can operate machinery which can print a pattern on cloth or cut a steel sheet with precision. Steam power meant that machines could do the work of man. It put machine-minders instead of craftsmen into the factories. Computer power is replacing the machine-minders by automation. This is probably the real power revolution of the late twentieth century.

Facts

★ The most powerful computer in the world can do over 30 million sums per second.

★ Computers are not foolproof. They only work if they have been correctly programmed. The programmes must be prepared by man. Since they are machines they need to be serviced and repaired by man if they make mistakes then it is the programmer or the service engineer or the manufacturer who is really at fault.

The Control Room of an automated foundry in Germany

Assignments

1. In the pictures on these pages you can see that despite automation man is still the controlling influence behind the machines. What new skills are required?

2. Are there any computers in your area? What are they used for? Is there one in the Town Hall or City Hall?

3. Find out how computers work. How can they be programmed to operate machines? What are the advantages of using computer-controlled machinery? Are there any disadvantages? Discuss this topic with your friends.

4. Another new source of power is the laser beam. This has been used in the tailoring industry as the laser beam can be made to trace an intricate pattern and cut many pieces of cloth at the same time where in the past hand-cutting methods could only manage one piece at a time. Find out more about the application of the laser beam to industry.

5. See if you can discover any new applications of power in modern industry.

Reading

Many new industrial products are developed each year. In most cases these are developments within particular industries such as the invention of a new type of pencil or the introduction of a new car model. Periodically new industries develop out of these innovations. The oil refining industry grew out of the invention and development of the motor vehicle and the aeroplane. Similarly the plastics industry has developed out of the oil refining industry. Plastics in their turn have given rise to a wide range of developments, from a revolution in the packaging industry and the production of polythene bags which have helped to make the deep freezing of food in the home a practical proposition, to the cheap manufacture of thousands of other products such as pens, table tops, gramophone records, car furnishings and television sets. Another important new industry has also grown out of oil refining and that is the manufacture of synthetic fibres like terylene. Other synthetic fibres have been produced and some have been derived from coal tar (nylon) or timber (rayon).

Facts

★ Polythene was discovered in 1933 – the year of the first synthetic detergents.

★ Nylon was discovered in 1935 and the first nylon stockings were sold in 1940.

★ Rayon is made from cellulose. The cellulose usually comes from wood pulp. The wood pulp is usually that of spruce pine.

★ Nylon was originally derived from coal tar but nowadays is usually made from petroleum by-products.

★ The first man-made fibres were on sale in France in 1889.

Assignments

1. Write about a 'Chemical Works' after looking closely at the photographs on the opposite page taken in three continents – South America (top left), Europe (bottom left), North America (right). Do you agree that the pipes, retorts and other characteristics of a chemical works make interesting patterns or do you think they are ugly?

2. Is there a chemcial works in your area? What does it produce?

3. How far is your life affected by the growth of the plastics and synthetic fibre industries? Make a survey of your home and the things you use. Imagine that all the plastics faded into thin air. What would you be left with? What proportion of your clothes are made from synthetic fibres?

4. The chemical, oil-refining and plastics industries have produced many significant advances in the standards of living of people all over the world. D.D.T. has eradicated malaria in many areas, new drugs have given life and health to millions, fertilisers have enabled food production to rise. What are the disadvantages?

Index by Place

Index by Time

Acknowledgements

I wish to record my thanks to those friends whose advice helped me in the preparation of this book and in particular to Peter Kesteven for drawing the maps, diagrams and pictures from my rough plans.
Acknowledgements are due to the following organisations for their kindness in supplying photographs, maps and other information:
The Society for Cultural Relations with the U.S.S.R.; The High Commissioner for New Zealand; The High Commissioner for India; The High Commissioner for Zambia; The Ford Motor Company; The Japan Information Centre; The Brazilian Embassy; The Central Office of Information, London; The Hong Kong Trade Development Council; The German Embassy; The Agent General for Western Australia; I.C.I. Limited, Plastics Division; Photographer Richard Woldendorp; Ontario House, London; The Science Museum; The Government of British Columbia; The British Museum; The London Museum; The Cotton Board; Manchester Public Libraries; The Walker Art Gallery, Liverpool; The Embassy of Israel; Esso Petroleum Company Ltd.; Joseph Needham *Clerks and Craftsmen in China,* Cambridge University Press.

© 1974
Philip A. Sauvain
ISBN 0 7175 0644 4
First published 1974 by Hulton Educational Publications Ltd., Raans Road, Amersham, Bucks.
Printed in Great Britain by Flarepath Printers Ltd., St. Albans, Herts.